Clouds, Rain, Clouds Again

Clouds, Rain, Clouds Again

By **Lawrence F. Lowery**

Illustrated by Betty Fraser

NSTA **Kids**
National Science Teachers Association
Arlington, Virginia

National Science Teachers Association

Claire Reinburg, Director
Jennifer Horak, Managing Editor
Andrew Cooke, Senior Editor
Amanda O'Brien, Associate Editor
Wendy Rubin, Associate Editor
Amy America, Book Acquisitions Coordinator

ART AND DESIGN
Will Thomas Jr., Director
Joseph Butera, Cover, Interior Design
Original illustrations by Betty Fraser

PRINTING AND PRODUCTION
Catherine Lorrain, Director

NATIONAL SCIENCE TEACHERS ASSOCIATION
David L. Evans, Executive Director
David Beacom, Publisher

1840 Wilson Blvd., Arlington, VA 22201
www.nsta.org/store
For customer service inquiries, please call 800-277-5300.

Lexile® measure: 590L

Library of Congress Cataloging-in-Publication Data
Lowery, Lawrence F.
  Clouds, rain, clouds again / by Lawrence F. Lowery ; illustrated by Betty Fraser.
    pages cm -- (I wonder why)
  Summary: "In Clouds, rain, clouds again, the reader receives a simplified picture of the water cycle: cloud formation, rain, evaporation, and condensation that forms clouds. Clouds, rain, clouds again is part of the I Wonder Why book series, written to ignite the curiosity of children in grades K-6 while encouraging them to become avid readers"--Provided by publisher.
  Audience: K to grade 3.
  ISBN 978-1-938946-12-7 (print) -- ISBN 978-1-938946-72-1 (e-book) 1. Clouds--Juvenile literature. 2. Hydrologic cycle--Juvenile literature. I. Fraser, Betty, illustrator. II. National Science Teachers Association. III. Title.
  QC921.35.L69 2013
  551.48--dc23
                                    2013020459

Cataloging-in-Publication Data are also available from the Library of Congress for the e-book.

Introduction

The *I Wonder Why* books are science books created specifically for young learners who are in their first years of school. The content for each book was chosen to be appropriate for youngsters who are beginning to construct knowledge of the world around them. These youngsters ask questions. They want to know about things. They are more curious than they will be when they are a decade older. Research shows that science is students' favorite subject when they enter school for the first time.

Science is both *what* we know and *how* we come to know it. What we know is the content knowledge that accumulates over time as scientists continue to explore the universe in which we live. How we come to know science is the set of thinking and reasoning processes we use to get answers to the questions and inquiries in which we are engaged.

Scientists learn by observing, comparing, and organizing the objects and ideas they are investigating. Children learn the same way. These thinking processes are among several inquiry behaviors that enable us to find out about our world and how it works. Observing, comparing, and organizing are fundamental to the more advanced thinking processes of relating, experimenting, and inferring.

The five books in this set of the *I Wonder Why* series focus on Earth science content. The materials of our Earth are mostly in the forms of solids (rocks and minerals), liquids (water), and gases (air). Inquiries about these materials are initiated by curiosity. When we don't know something about an area of interest, we try to understand it by asking questions and doing investigations. These five Earth science books are written from the learner's point of view: *How Does the Wind Blow?*; *Clouds, Rain, Clouds Again*; *Spenser and the Rocks*; *Environments of Our Earth*; and *Up, Up in a Balloon*. Children inquire about pebbles and rocks, rain and wind, and jungles and deserts. Their curiosity leads them to ask questions about land forms, weather, and climate.

The information in these books leads the characters and the reader to discover how wind can be measured and how powerful it can be, how the water cycle works, that living things need water to survive, and that plants and animals have adapted to different climate-related environments. They also learn how people have learned to fly in the ocean of air that surrounds Earth.

Each book uses a different approach to take the reader through simple scientific information. One book is expository, providing factual information. Several are narratives that allow a story to unfold. Another provides a historical perspective that tells how we gradually learn science through experimentations over time. The combination of different artwork, literary perspectives, and scientific knowledge brings the content to the reader through several instructional avenues.

In addition, the content in these books correlates to criteria set forth by national standards. Often the content is woven into each book so that its presence is subtle but powerful. The science activities in the Parent/Teacher Handbook section in each book enable learners to carry out their own investigations that relate to the content of the book. The materials needed for these activities are easily obtained, and the activities have been tested with youngsters to be sure they are age appropriate.

After students have completed a science activity, rereading or referring back to the book and talking about connections with the activity can be a deepening experience that stabilizes the learning as a long-term memory.

Have you ever looked up at the sky and watched clouds float by?

Sometimes the clouds are so thin that you can almost see through them.

When these high, thin clouds are in the sky,
it is almost always a very fine day.

On a bright, sunny day, look above you.
You can sometimes see flat clouds
that stay smooth and bright.

When these clouds are in the sky,
chances are that it will not rain.

Have you ever seen clouds like these?
They look like balls of cotton in the sky.

You may be able to see many things
when you look at these clouds.
You may see make-believe ships and castles.
You may see giant faces.

Sometimes these puffy clouds change.
They get dark and gray.
This tells you a rainstorm may be
coming your way.

Sometimes when you look up you see a gray sky and dark clouds.
They even hide the Sun. On such a day, it is almost sure to rain.

You hear thunder. Thunder makes the air shake and tremble.
Maybe the sky lights up when lightning leaps across the sky.
When this happens, down from the clouds come the thunderstorm rains.

You may not like a rainy day.
But rain is water, and water is needed.
The water we drink once fell from the clouds.
The water we use for washing and swimming
also came down to us as rain.

Trees and bushes need water that falls as rain. Grasses and shrubs, mushrooms and ferns need the water that comes from rain.

Every living plant needs water.
Every living plant needs rain.

Animals in the forest need water to drink.
Animals in the fields need water too.

Every animal, large or small, needs
the water that falls as rain.
Everything that lives needs water.

The water that flows in rivers and streams
once fell from the clouds as rain.

The water that fills the lakes and ponds comes from the clouds as rain.

The water that flows over rocks,
the water that splashes and tumbles,
the water that splatters and spills—
all once fell from the clouds as rain.

Ponds and puddles, oceans and seas
all get their water from rain.

Where do clouds get water?
How does rain get into the sky?

When a puddle dries up, water goes into the air.
Most water evaporates into the air.

High in the air, this water forms clouds.

Sometimes the water in the clouds forms drops.

When large drops form, they fall down to Earth as rain.

So you see, we must have clouds to bring us rain.
There must be water to make clouds again.

Parent/Teacher Handbook

Introduction

Clouds, Rain, Clouds Again gives the reader a simplified picture of the water cycle: cloud formation, rain, evaporation, and condensation that forms clouds.

Inquiry Processes

Observing cloud shapes, cloud altitude, and the evaporation of water from ponds, lakes, and other bodies of water is the central scientific content stressed in this book. Observations over a period of time in varying weather conditions will help the reader fully appreciate each part of the water cycle.

Content

The cyclical movement of water from the clouds to Earth as rain and from bodies of water back into the air as water vapor, which condenses into clouds again, is a simplified version of the water cycle.

Clouds are classified by their form or shape and altitude. The three major types are cirrus, cumulus, and stratus. Cirrus means curls or ringlets. These filmy clouds are thin and feathery white. They are seen high in the air on fair days (20,000–40,000 feet). Cumulus clouds are massive piles of clouds with flat bases and cotton-ball tops that resemble fleece. They range from 4,000 to 20,000 feet in altitude. When the cumulus cloud turns dark, condensation is occurring in the cloud. Stratus clouds are low-hanging sheets, gray in color, that cover the entire sky like fog. They form at altitudes around 1,500 to 4,000 feet.

Cirrus

Cumulus

Stratus

Science Activities

Observing That Water Evaporates

Place containers with openings of varying sizes on a shelf or windowsill. Put the same amount of water in each container. Mark the starting water level on each container, and take measurements at the same time every day. Make a simple bar graph of the evaporation rate for each container. Which container has the highest evaporation rate? What does this tell you about evaporation as it relates to exposed surface areas? Are there other factors besides the amount of exposed water surface that affects the evaporation rate? Clouds are formed when the evaporated water in the atmosphere condenses.

Making a Model of the Water Cycle

Water on Earth evaporates into the atmosphere as moisture; moisture in the atmosphere may condense and return to Earth. To make a model of this cycle, inflate a large, transparent plastic bag and fit it over a wide-mouth jar or an aquarium filled halfway with water. Prop up or suspend the bag. Observe the bag from time to time. You will see that droplets of moisture appear on the top and sides of the bag, collect, and run down into the container. What you see is analogous to the natural water cycle.

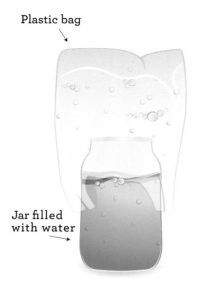

Plastic bag

Jar filled with water

Observing How Clouds Are Formed

Obtain two identical wide-mouth jars. Line half of the inside of each jar with soft, black cloth as shown. Add glue to hold the cloth in place, then carefully soak the cloth with water. Cover each jar with a square of plastic or glass and set them upright, one in a pan of cold water and the other in a pan of very hot water. Leave the jars in the pans for 15 minutes. Remove them from the pans and set the cold jar upside down over the warm jar, leaving the plastic squares over the openings. Hold a flashlight to shine down through both jars, then carefully remove the plastic squares. A cloud will form as the cold air in the top jar flows down into the bottom jar and pushes the warm, moist air upward and into contact with the cooler air.

— Flashlight

— Cold jar

— Black cloth glued to sides of jars and saturated with water

— Plastic square

— Warm jar

Experiments can be done with these jars: Repeat the activity after reversing the positions of the jars. Tiny tissue paper streamers can be placed inside the jars. The streamers will indicate the direction in which the air flows.

Based on the experiments, observe cloud formations and imagine the relationship between hot and cold air masses.

Measuring the Size of Raindrops

On a rainy day, pour some flour through a sifter into a pie pan until the flour is 1/2 in. (1 cm) deep. Cover the pan with a large plate and take it outdoors. Hold the pan in the rain, uncover it, and let the rain fall into the flour for 3 seconds. Re-cover the pan and go inside. When you uncover the pan, you will see wet, round lumps where the raindrops fell. Let the lumps dry, then use the sifter to separate the lumps from the flour. Measure the lumps with a ruler or seriate them by size to learn about the relative size of raindrops. (*Note:* The lumps are slightly larger than actual raindrops.)

If you keep records, you can compare the sizes of raindrops at different times during a storm or between different storms. You can also compare samples from different locales.